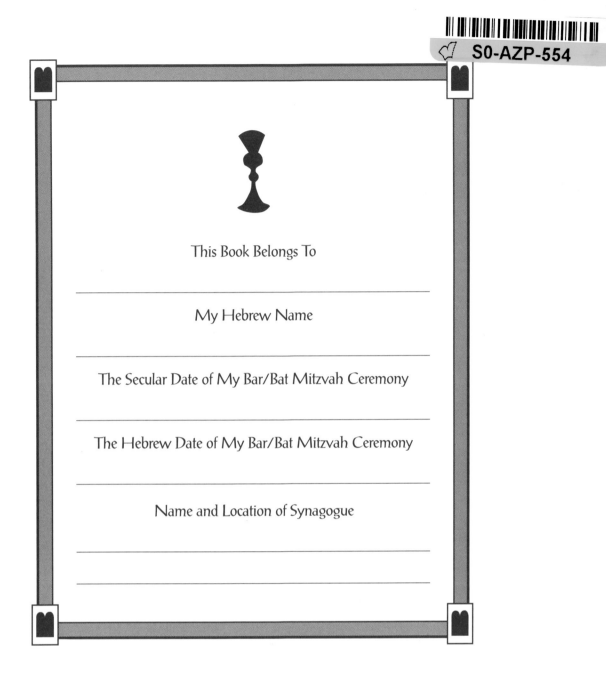

This Book Belongs To

_____

My Hebrew Name

_____

The Secular Date of My Bar/Bat Mitzvah Ceremony

_____

The Hebrew Date of My Bar/Bat Mitzvah Ceremony

_____

Name and Location of Synagogue

_____

_____

66 When a Jewish child reads from the Torah, he or she is
enveloped in its heritage, in its power, in the majesty of Sinai.
He or she says to the community: 'I am now thirteen years old.
I am now ready to fulfill the covenant with God by being responsible
for performing *mitzvot*, the obligations of Jewish life.' 99

—*Putting God on the Guest List*

The Bar/Bat Mitzvah Memory Book

An Album for
Treasuring the Spiritual Celebration

RABBI JEFFREY K. SALKIN & NINA SALKIN

JEWISH LIGHTS Publishing
Woodstock, Vermont

Dedicated to our mothers, Sidonia Karpel Salkin, of blessed memory, and Isabelle Rubin, who never had the opportunity to become bat mitzvah. To our fathers, George Salkin and Mel Rubin, who were bar mitzvah and who wish that it had been a different kind of experience. To our sons, Sam and Gabriel, who are doing it "our way," and, we pray, "their way."

Acknowledgments

We appreciate all the hard work of Sandra Korinchak, Martha McKinney, and Emily Wichland, who shepherded this project along. Our inspiration continues to be Stuart Matlins, Publisher of Jewish Lights, who realized the need for this book and invited us to create it.

We are deeply grateful to our summer Berkshires *havurah*—the Goldsteins, Karps, and Spungen-Bildner families. Over the past ten years, we have thought out loud together about our children's *b'nei mitzvah*, and we have dreamed together about a Jewish world where God, Torah, and *mitzvot* might assume center stage.

The Bar/Bat Mitzvah Memory Book:
An Album for Treasuring the Spiritual Celebration

© 2001 by Jeffrey K. Salkin and Nina Salkin

10 9 8 7 6 5 4 3 2 1

This book is printed on acid-free paper.
Manufactured in Hong Kong
Cover design: Bronwen Battaglia
Text design: Chelsea Cloeter

Jewish Lights Publishing
A Division of LongHill Partners, Inc.
Sunset Farm Offices, Route 4, P.O. Box 237
Woodstock, VT 05091
Tel: (802) 457-4000   Fax: (802) 457-4004
www.jewishlights.com

Contents

Introduction

What Makes This Bar/Bat Mitzvah Memory Book Different from All Other Memory Books?

A few weeks ago, we sent our younger son, Gabriel, to Jewish overnight camp for the first time. As we unpacked his duffel bag and made his bed, we both felt a lump in our throats. True, this trip to camp meant that Gabriel was now mature enough to handle two weeks of nights without us. And it also meant that we were no longer as young as we once were.

We took a photograph of him with his bunkmates. We gave him a big hug and then drove away, reflecting on this bittersweet moment in our lives.

There is something sacred about all this. Our friend Joel Grishaver, Jewish educator and author, once advocated the idea of starting a Jewish photo album for each child. When your child is born, buy a photo album with empty plastic sheets. Use a labeling machine to create labels for each page: "First day at Jewish nursery school." "First day of religious school." "First time giving *tzedakah*." "First time going to Jewish camp." "Getting on the plane to Israel for the first time." And then, he said, take the pictures. You already have the pages labeled for them. Just live your Jewish life in such a way that you will be able to witness those scenes and remember them.

That's what makes this bar/bat mitzvah memory book different from all other memory books.

It is an exercise in "pre-memory." Parents, by looking through the pages in this book, and seeing the kinds of memories your child might have and might consider worth remembering forever, you and your child can actually plan those experiences and, therefore—if such a thing is possible—"plan" those special feelings of memory that will endure. Because those memories are, in fact, holy.

This is your road map for bar/bat mitzvah. It will help you know what to expect and what the major holy sites are on the sacred journey through this important moment of Jewish life. It will help you not to miss the spiritual highlights of bar/bat mitzvah—highlights that can be kept alive each day of your life *after* the ceremony.

Many families are looking for ways to make the bar/bat mitzvah experience richer and deeper. To help you do that, you may wish to use this book along with *Putting God on the Guest List: How to Reclaim the Spiritual Meaning of Your Child's Bar or Bat Mitzvah* and *For Kids—Putting God on Your Guest List: How to Claim the Spiritual Meaning of Your Bar or Bat Mitzvah* (both published by Jewish Lights). You will learn how to plan to remember the significant moments in this sacred rite of passage.

We once knew a religious school teacher who had a family Bible with the names of everyone in the family inscribed in it—going all the way back to 1400s Spain! Imagine how you would feel if your own ancestors had kept a careful record of everyone in their own families. With this memory book, you can create a keepsake that will become a family heirloom to last through the years.

This memory book will help you see yourself as part of a rich history that includes your family and that goes beyond your family. The Hebrew term for memory, *zachor*, is used 169 times in the Torah. The square root of 169 is 13, the age of becoming bar/bat mitzvah. Memory is the square root of everything we do in Jewish life.

Mazal tov!

Rabbi Jeffrey K. Salkin   Nina Salkin

Who
Am I
and
What
Am I?

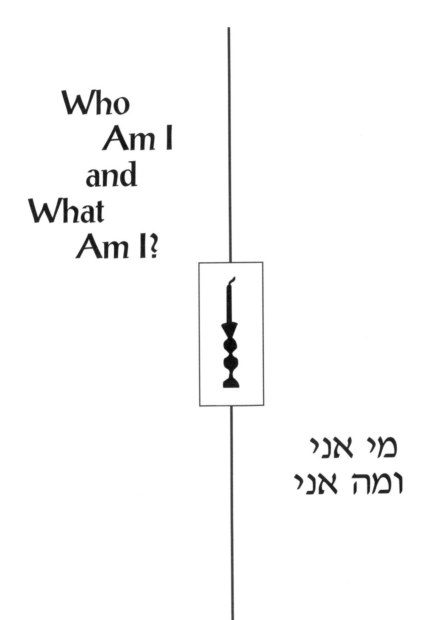

מי אני
ומה אני

66 There is no such thing as a bar or bat mitzvah ceremony
without tears.

The tears belong to several people.
They belong to parents who are swelling with pride and relief.

They belong to grandparents who may come up for their *aliyah.*
They listen to their grandchild read or chant from the Torah,
and by the time they utter the closing blessing,
their lips are quivering and their tears are falling.

I have seen tears fall right onto the Torah scroll.

Of all the places where tears might fall,
that is the holiest place of all. 99

—*Putting God on the Guest List*

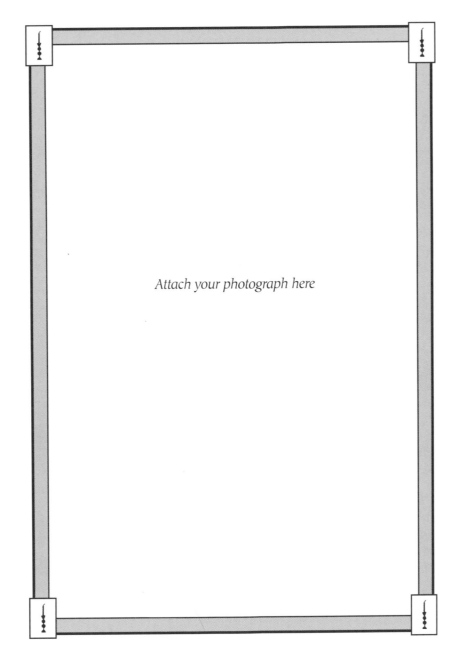

Attach your photograph here

I am named for:

_____   _____
NAME/RELATION   NAME/RELATION

These are their qualities that I would like to emulate:

_____   _____

_____   _____

9

My Family

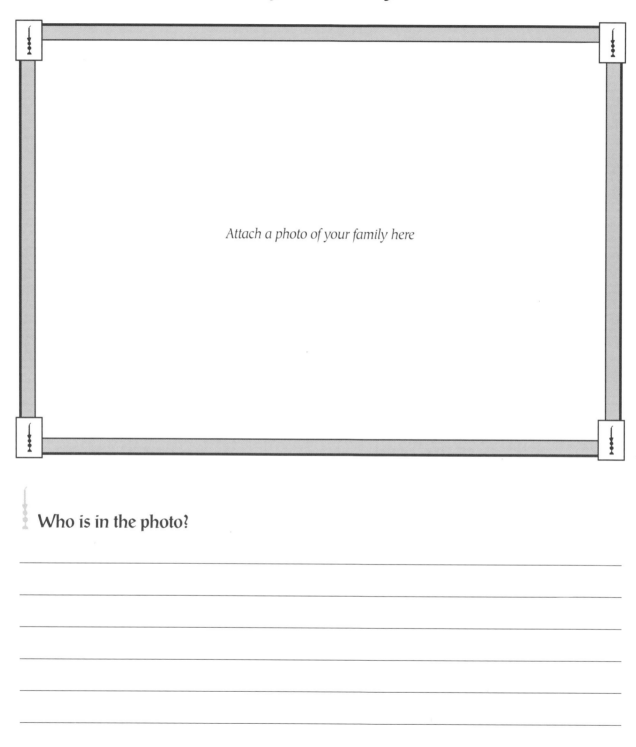

Attach a photo of your family here

Who is in the photo?

_____

_____

_____

_____

_____

_____

_____

My Family Tree

Draw your family tree and attach it here

66 The spiritual life of the family begins when we reclaim our past.
If we have forgotten our Hebrew names, we must try to remember them.
If we have forgotten our parents' Hebrew names,
we must try to remember them.
If we have forgotten the holy qualities of the great-aunts and uncles
for whom we were named,
we must try to remember them.
If we have forgotten the names of the cities in Europe
where our families came from
and the names of the great teachers of those cities,
we must try to remember them. 99

—*Putting God on the Guest List*

66 These are the names
of the children of Israel … 99

—Exodus 1:1

What do my grandparents remember about when they became bar or bat mitzvah?

_____ remembers:

NAME OF GRANDPARENT

The name of the synagogue: _____

It was located in: _____ Date of the ceremony: _____

The names of the rabbi, cantor, or other people
who helped them prepare for their bar or bat mitzvah: _____

_____

The Torah portion: _____

Special memory of ceremony: _____

_____

_____

_____ remembers:

NAME OF GRANDPARENT

The name of the synagogue: _____

It was located in: _____ Date of the ceremony: _____

The names of the rabbi, cantor, or other people
who helped them prepare for their bar or bat mitzvah: _____

_____

The Torah portion: _____

Special memory of ceremony: _____

_____

_____

_____ remembers:

The name of the synagogue: _____

It was located in: _____ Date of the ceremony: _____

The names of the rabbi, cantor, or other people
who helped them prepare for their bar or bat mitzvah: _____

_____

The Torah portion: _____

Special memory of ceremony: _____

_____

_____

_____ remembers:

The name of the synagogue: _____

It was located in: _____ Date of the ceremony: _____

The names of the rabbi, cantor, or other people
who helped them prepare for their bar or bat mitzvah: _____

_____

The Torah portion: _____

Special memory of ceremony: _____

_____

_____

66 The Talmud teaches that
to hear your child's child reading Torah
is like hearing the words from Sinai itself. 99

—*Putting God on the Guest List*

"When I became bar mitzvah,
my grandfather came to me one night
in a vision
and gave me another soul
in exchange for mine.
Ever since then,
I have been a different person."

—Shalom of Belz, Hasidic teacher

Go Forth
from the Land
of Childhood

לך לך מארעך
וממלדתך
ומבית אביך

66 Bar and bat mitzvah is about ritual maturity.
It is about growing up as a Jew.
It is about becoming a fuller member of the Jewish community.
But it is also about moral responsibility,
about connecting to Torah, to community, to God. **99**

—*Putting God on the Guest List*

66 Jewish children become bar or bat mitzvah
because of God's covenant with the people of Israel.
The *mitzvot* are our end of the covenant.
Mitzvah, in fact, is one of the most important ideas
Judaism gave to the world:
A relationship with God entails mutual responsibility.
Traditionally, there are 613 *mitzvot* derived from the Torah.
The idea of *mitzvah* is central to Jewish identity:
It is the essence of the Covenant,
our end of the agreement made at Sinai,
the summit of Jewish existence. **99**

—*Putting God on the Guest List*

Why am I having this ceremony?

_____

_____

_____

_____

What do I want to remember about my bar/bat mitzvah experience?

_____

_____

_____

_____

These are the *mitzvot* that I performed to prepare to become bar or bat mitzvah (see *For Kids—Putting God on Your Guest List* for a list of *mitzvah* project ideas):

_____

_____

_____

_____

_____

_____

I contributed to these *tzedakot* (see *Putting God on the Guest List* for a list of *tzedakot* ideas):

_____

_____

My mother and father have special blessings for me.

My mother says that she wants me to always be proud to be Jewish because:

_____

_____

_____

_____

My father says that he wants me to always be proud to be Jewish because:

_____

_____

_____

_____

" A generation
can only receive the teachings
if it renews them.
We do not take
unless we also give. "

—Martin Buber, twentieth-century Jewish teacher

And
This
Is
the Torah

וזאת
התורה

66 The service is carefully and deliberately orchestrated
to take us, ultimately, from the mundane planes of our lives
to the heights of Sinai—and beyond.

This liturgical choreography may seem strange or esoteric
or irrelevant and beyond your experience.
But it is weighted with millennia of
Jewish experience and wisdom and hopes.
Not the least of these hopes and aspirations is that you,
who are now of the age where you can fully appreciate the service,
will feel its full force and know, in the depths of your youthful soul,
what it means to be a Jew who can ascend the mountain of prayers
to a summit where every religiously curious Jew
has climbed before. **99**

—*Putting God on the Guest List*

🕮 My Torah portion is:

_____

It is from:

_____

My favorite verse is:

_____

_____

_____

🕮 My *haftarah* is from:

_____

My favorite verse is:

_____

_____

_____

> 66 The Torah scroll is not vocalized
>   to allow the wise to give his own voice to the text.
> This is what keeps the Torah eternal
>   and what keeps the congregation alive. 99

—Rabbi David ben Abi Zimra, medieval Spanish Jewish sage

My Devar Torah

Print it out and attach it here.

Judaism says that thirteen is the age of spiritual and moral choices. Some rabbinic sources say that only upon turning thirteen is a youth first able to make mature choices, because then the child becomes endowed with both the *yetzer hara* (the evil inclination, which urges us to be selfish and not look at the moral issues behind our actions) and the *yetzer hatov* (the good inclination), the dueling forces that Jewish theology perceives are within each of us. Now, you can begin to ascend to the good and the holy, and start making ethical decisions.

What are some ethical and moral issues that you expect to confront over the next few years? Which Jewish principles do you hope to draw on when you make your choices about each? For example:

> *Shabbat:* Honoring the Sabbath
> *Gemilut Chasadim:* Acts of Loving-Kindness
> *Talmud Torah:* The Study of Torah
> *Kedushat Halashon:* The Holiness of Speech
> *Tzar Baalei Chayim:* Noncruelty to Animals
> *Hidur P'nai Zakein:* Honoring the Elderly
> *Kol Yisrael Arevim:* All Jews Are Responsible for Each Other
> *Tikkun Atzmi:* Repairing the Self
> *Tikkun Olam:* Repairing the World

_____

_____

_____

_____

_____

_____

_____

_____

_____

From All
My Teachers
I Have
Gained
Wisdom

מכל
מלמדי
הסכלתי

❝ As a teenager in my synagogue recently said:

    'A Judaism
    that doesn't ask you to make any changes in your life
            is not Judaism.'

    So instead of just 'coasting through' Judaism,
imagine a Judaism that asks us
        to make changes in our lives.
    Moreover, *demand* a Judaism
     that requires such changes.
        Anything less is not Judaism. **❞**

—For Kids—Putting God on Your Guest List

My rabbi(s):

_____
NAME(S) OF RABBI(S)

Ask your rabbi(s) to answer below:

What Jewish values are most important to you? What special Jewish teachings do you want me to remember?

_____

_____

_____

_____

My cantor(s):

_____
NAME(S) OF CANTOR(S)

Ask your cantor(s) to answer below:

What Jewish values are most important to you? What special Jewish teachings do you want me to remember?

_____

_____

_____

_____

**" Get yourself a rabbi,
and acquire for yourself
a study companion. "**

—Pirke Avot

27

👁 I have a special religious school teacher, director of education, or youth leader who has helped me grow up as a young Jew.

This person's name is:

_____

Ask this person to answer below:
What Jewish values are most important to you? What special Jewish teachings do you want me to remember?

_____

_____

_____

👁 These are the names of the congregation leaders who participated in my ceremony:

_____

_____

Ask these congregation leaders to answer below:
Why do you love our synagogue? What do you love about Judaism? Why do you want Judaism to continue?

_____

_____

_____

_____

❝ May your heart be filled
                    with intuition
        and your words
                be filled with insight. ❞

—Talmud

Come
Before God
with
Rejoicing

באו לפניו
ברינה

> 66 The scroll was returned to the ark
> with song and procession,
> and the service was resumed.
> No thunder sounded,
> no lightning struck.
> The institution of bat mitzvah
> had been born without incident,
> and the rest of the day was all rejoicing. 99

—Judith Kaplan Eisenstein, describing her May 1922
bat mitzvah ceremony (the first in North America)

🖋 Who led the service?

_____

🖋 Who else said something special to me?

_____

I remember these words (from rabbis, cantors, or congregation leaders):

_____

_____

_____

_____

🖋 Who else did something special for me?

_____

What was done for me?

_____

Gift(s) I received from the congregation:

_____

_____

66 May songs of praise
          ever be upon your tongue
     and your vision
          a straight path before you. 99

—Talmud

Attach photographs of the rehearsal and/or ceremony.
Tell what is happening in each photograph.

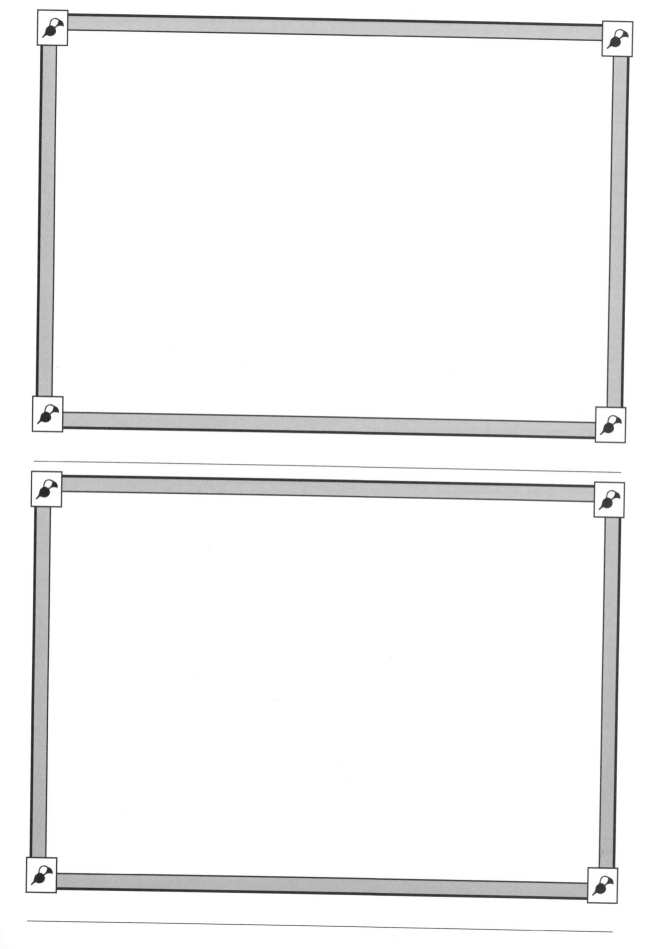

At the Shabbat dinner before my bar/bat mitzvah ceremony, the following people had special honors or offered special words:

_____

_____

_____

_____

_____

I remember that these are some of the things they said:

_____

_____

_____

_____

_____

_____

66 One thread links all the bar and bat mitzvah ceremonies
throughout history,
all the comings of age of every Jewish boy from Abraham on
and of every Jewish girl from Sarah on.
Bar and bat mitzvah means that you now are responsible for
fulfilling the *mitzvot* of Jewish ritual.
It is about growing up as a Jew.
It is about becoming a fuller member of the Jewish community.
It is about moral responsibility,
about connecting to Torah, to community, to God. **99**

—*For Kids—Putting God on Your Guest List*

🖋 I received some special gifts for my life as a Jewish adult:

_____ gave me a *tallit.*

_____ gave me a *kippah.*

_____ gave me *tefilin.*

_____ gave me _____.

_____ gave me _____.

_____ gave me _____.

If any of these objects have a special story, write about it here:

_____

_____

_____

_____

_____

_____

**❝ All relatives contributed
to the outfit
of the Bar Mitzvah boy. ❞**

—Caption for a photograph of
a bar mitzvah boy in Poland in the 1930s,
taken by the famous photographer Roman Vishniac

Honors

Who opened the ark during the service?

_____

Who had *aliyot*?

_____   _____

_____   _____

_____   _____

_____   _____

Who did *hagbah* (lifting the Torah)? _____

Who did *gelilah* (dressing the Torah)? _____

Who held the Torah? _____

Who else had honors during the service? What were these honors?

_____   _____

_____   _____

Who did *Kiddush* at the celebration? _____

Who did *Motzi*? _____

      “ At such moments we understand the Torah blessing.

Baruch attah Adonai, notein hatorah,

'Blessed are You, Adonai, Giver of the Torah.'

God did not just give Torah at Sinai. God gives Torah today.

This is Torah's magical potency that has spoken through the ages. **”**

—Putting God on the Guest List

To me, the most meaningful parts of the service were:

_____

_____

_____

What prayer from the service did you find most meaningful?

Copy it from your prayerbook and attach it here.

The music or songs I found most meaningful were:

_____

_____

_____

❝ There is an angel with a thousand heads.
Each head has a thousand mouths.
Each mouth has a thousand tongues.
Each tongue has a thousand songs.
Imagine the beauty of this angel's prayers. ❞

—Rebbe Nachman of Breslov, Hasidic teacher

37

🖋 **This page is for your parents to fill out.**

In traditional Judaism, parents say a prayer when their child becomes bar or bat mitzvah.

This is what it is:

ברוך שפטרני מעונשו של זה

Baruch she-petarani me-onsho shel zeh.

"Blessed is the One Who has now freed me from responsibility for this child."

You are not freed from *all* responsibility for your new teenager's behavior, but how do you want your child to use his or her new maturity?

_____

_____

_____

_____

_____

_____

> ❝ An important part of becoming bar or bat mitzvah
> is growing as an individual.
> Ancient rabbis believed that the ultimate goal of the *mitzvot*
> was nothing less than *letzaref haberiot,*
> turning someone into a better person. ❞

—*For Kids—Putting God on Your Guest List*

Joy
and
Gladness

שמחה
וששון

66 The peak moments of life,
when we experience the drama of passage,
have an uncanny way of bringing us home.
They can take us out of exile
and show us the Jerusalem of the soul.
They remind us that our lives
have a rhythm and a purpose. 99

—*Putting God on the Guest List*

Attach your invitation here.

A place for your guests to sign or write their wishes for you.

_____

_____

_____

_____

_____

_____

_____

_____

_____

_____

_____

_____

_____

_____

_____

_____

_____

_____

_____

_____

**" Judaism begins with *the* Torah.
But ideally,
Torah can become
the way you view yourself as a Jew. "**

—For Kids—Putting God on Your Guest List

_____

_____

_____

_____

_____

_____

_____

_____

_____

_____

_____

_____

_____

_____

_____

_____

66 Torah continues into our own day.
As *Pirke Avot* (the ethical teachings of the ancient rabbis) says,
'Every day a voice goes forth from Sinai'—
every day, at least,
if we turn down the noise of the world
and train our ears to hear the truth
and the beauty of the Torah. **99**

—*For Kids—Putting God on Your Guest List*

Clear
a Pathway
through
the Wilderness
of Life

פנו דרך
במדבר

66 The religious individual can never sit still.
He or she is always packing up the tent,
    moving through the wilderness of life,
and remembering that there is
    a Promised Land of the soul. 99

—*Putting God on the Guest List*

My plans for my Jewish future: ✓

☐ To continue religious school
☐ To decide who my favorite Jewish authors are and to learn from them
☐ To join my synagogue youth group
☐ To volunteer in my Jewish community or synagogue
☐ To go to a Jewish summer camp
☐ To go on a trip to Israel

☐ _____

☐ _____

I plan to learn more about: ✓

☐ Jewish history
☐ The Holocaust (Shoah)
☐ Israel
☐ Women's contributions to Judaism
☐ Jewish prayer
☐ Jewish thought

☐ Social justice issues from a Jewish point of view
☐ Mysticism
☐ Meditation
☐ Jewish music
☐ Jewish art
☐ Jewish dance

☐ _____
☐ _____

Mitzvot and acts of tikkun olam (repairing the world) that I want to do:

_____

_____

_____

_____

> "Let young people know that
> every deed counts,
> that every word has power.
> Let them remember to build a life
> as if it were a work of art."

—Abraham Joshua Heschel,
twentieth-century Jewish theologian and philosopher

Helpful resources for keeping the spiritual meaning in bar and bat mitzvah

Putting God on the Guest List
How to Reclaim the Spiritual Meaning of Your Child's Bar or Bat Mitzvah

by Rabbi Jeffrey K. Salkin (Reform)

Foreword by Rabbi Sandy Eisenberg Sasso (Reconstructionist)
Introduction by Rabbi William H. Lebeau (Conservative)

Helps people find core spiritual values in American Jewry's most misunderstood ceremony. How did bar and bat mitzvah originate? What is its lasting significance? What are the ethics of celebration? **Shows how to make the event more spiritually meaningful,** to help both parent and child truly be there when the moment of Sinai is recreated in their lives. 6 x 9, 224 pp., Quality PB, ISBN 1-879045-59-1 $16.95

66 I hope every family planning a bar or bat mitzvah celebration reads Rabbi Salkin's book. 99 —Rabbi Harold S. Kushner, author of *When Bad Things Happen to Good People*

For Kids—Putting God on Your Guest List
How to Claim the Spiritual Meaning of Your Bar or Bat Mitzvah

by Rabbi Jeffrey K. Salkin

An informative, lighthearted, inspiring, and instructive guide for kids as they embark upon a journey of growth, self-discovery, and exploration in preparation for their bar or bat mitzvah. Engages and inspires in a language young people can understand, to teach them the core spiritual values of Judaism. 6 x 9, 144 pp., Quality PB, ISBN 1-58023-015-6 $14.95

66 We've used *Putting God on the Guest List* in our b'nai mitzvah program for many years. I've always wished for a companion book that could talk to the kids themselves. This is the book I've been waiting for! 99

—Rabbi Laura Geller, Temple Emanuel, Beverly Hills, California

66 A great resource for kids with every kind of Jewish background, even if you are a kid with two parents who are rabbis—like me! I would recommend this book to my friends, my younger brother and sister, my cousins, and everyone I know who will become bar or bat mitzvah. 99 —Joshua Zecher Ross, Age 13, Bar Mitzvah Parshat Noah 5759

Available from your bookstore
or directly from Jewish Lights Publishing at 800-962-4544.